ONE-OF-A-KIND
M O M

Rebecca Germany

HUMBLECREEK
INSPIRATION FOR LIFE

Mom—
a simple little word that
conjures up fond memories,
warm feelings, and a sense
of wonder at all she
manages to accomplish. . .

M–O–M

When it comes to love, Mom's the word.

AUTHOR UNKNOWN

4

MAKER OF MEMORIES

There was a place in childhood that I remember well,
And there a voice of sweetest tone bright fairy tales did tell.
SAMUEL LOVER, "MY MOTHER DEAR"

Manufacturer of Miracles

Mother love is the fuel that
enables a normal human being to do the impossible.

Author Unknown

MISTRESS
OF THE MANOR

It is not our exalted feelings,
it is our sentiments that build the necessary home.

ELIZABETH BOWEN

MINDER OF MANNERS

The mother's heart is the child's schoolroom.

HENRY WARD BEECHER

MOLDER OF MINDS

People are what their mothers make them.

RALPH WALDO EMERSON

Meter of Money

The greatest teacher is not experience;
it is example.

John Croyle

MODEL
OF MATURITY

There is only one way to bring up a child
in the way he should go
and that is to travel that way yourself.

ABRAHAM LINCOLN

MEGAPHONE OVER MAYHEM

That energy which makes a child hard to manage
is the energy which afterwards
makes him a manager of life.

HENRY WARD BEECHER

MOUTHPIECE
OF THE MUTE

A mother understands
what a child does not say.

JEWISH PROVERB

MIGHTY
OVER MALADY

Mother is the bank where
we deposit all our hurts and worries.

AUTHOR UNKNOWN

MENDER
OF MALFUNCTION

A mother's love for her child

is like nothing else in the world.

It knows no law, no pity,

it dares all things and crushes down remorselessly

all that stands in its path.

AGATHA CHRISTIE

MASTER
OF MOTIVATION

No influence is so powerful as that of the mother.

SARAH JOSEPHA HALE

MOTIVATOR OF MORALE

If you can give your son or daughter only one gift,
let it be enthusiasm.

BRUCE BARTON

MILD OVER MISTAKES

The heart of a mother is
a deep abyss at the bottom of which
you will always find forgiveness.

HONORÉ DE BALZAC

Marker of a Moment

The work will wait while you show your child the rainbow,
but the rainbow won't wait while you do the work.

Patricia Clafford

Misty Over the Miniscule

Holy as heaven a mother's tender love,
the love of many prayers and many tears which
changes not with dim, declining years.

Caroline Norton

MOVER OF MOUNTAINS

To describe my mother would be
to write about a hurricane in its perfect power.

MAYA ANGELOU

Mediator
of the Master

I remember my mother's prayers
and they have always followed me.
They have clung to me all my life.

ABRAHAM LINCOLN

MONITOR OF MORALS

The conscience of children is formed by
the influences that surround them;
their notions of good and evil are
the result of the moral atmosphere they breathe.

JEAN PAUL RICHTER

Meekest of the Meek

When you lead your sons and daughters in the good way,
let your words be tender and caressing,
in terms of discipline that wins the heart's assent.

Elijah Ben Solomon Zalman

MAINSTAY OF MANY

A mother is she who can take the place of all others
but whose place no one else can take.

CARDINAL MERMILLOD

MOM

MOM = a load of responsibility.

And you think mothers had it better in the Good Ol' Days?

Washboards vs. washing machines
Clotheslines vs. dryers
Butter churns vs. margarine tubs
Smokehouses vs. delis
Telegraphs vs. cell phones
Rug beaters vs. vacuums
Oil lamps vs. electric lights
Cooking fires vs. microwaves
Horses and buggies vs. SUVs
River water vs. bottled water
Snake oil vs. medical technology
Midwives vs. modern maternity ward

History has produced millions of mothers, but I'm so glad I had you.

Sarah
may have mothered a nation,
but she couldn't have
managed your brood.

The hand that rocks the cradle
rules the nation and its destiny.

SOUTH AFRICAN PROVERB

Mom

Moses' mother
may have been brave enough to set her baby afloat in the river,
but you were brave enough to send me to kindergarten.

The mother-child relationship is paradoxical and,
in a sense, tragic.
It requires the most intense love on the mother's side,
yet this very love must help the child grow
away from the mother,
and to become fully independent.

ERICH FROMM

Mom

Hannah

may have been dedicated enough
to let her son grow up at the temple,
but you were dedicated enough
to put up with me every day.

Children are the sum of what
mothers contribute to their lives.

AUTHOR UNKNOWN

Susanna Wesley

may have passed her faith on to
two of history's greatest evangelists
who impacted the lives of millions,
but you impacted my life by passing on your faith to me.

My mother was the source from which I derived
the guiding principles of my life.

JOHN WESLEY

Shakespeare's mother may have raised a literary genius, but she didn't get to raise me as you did.

There was never a great man
who had not a great mother.

OLIVE SCHREINER

George Washington's and Abraham Lincoln's

mothers may have raised remarkable presidents,
but you raised a remarkable me.

All that I am or hope to be
I owe to my angel mother.

ABRAHAM LINCOLN

All I am I owe to my mother.
I attribute all my success in life to the
moral, intellectual, and physical education
I received from her.

GEORGE WASHINGTON

MOM

Anna Jarvis's

mother may have inspired her daughter to get
an official Mother's Day established,
but she only got it done before I could.

Nothing you do for children is ever wasted.
They seem not to notice us, hovering, averting our eyes,
and they seldom offer thanks,
but what we do for them is never wasted.

GARRISON KEILLOR

TV moms of the 50s
may have had perfect hairdos,
but they weren't huggable like you.

Some are kissing mothers
and some are scolding mothers,
but it is love just the same,
and most mothers kiss and scold together.

PEARL S. BUCK

Of all the mothers,
you are the best.
Who can I really
compare you to
but the woman in Proverbs?

She gets up while it is still dark;
she provides food for her family
and portions for her servant girls.

PROVERBS 31:15

She opens her arms to the poor
and extends her hands to the needy.

PROVERBS 31:20

She is clothed with strength and dignity;
she can laugh at the days to come.

PROVERBS 31:25

She speaks with wisdom,
and faithful instruction is on her tongue.

PROVERBS 31:26

She watches over the affairs of her household
and does not eat the bread of idleness.

PROVERBS 31:27

Her children arise and call her blessed.

PROVERBS 31:28

Mom

A man loves his sweetheart the most,
his wife the best, but his mother the longest.

IRISH PROVERB

What the mother sings to the cradle
goes all the way to the coffin.

HENRY WARD BEECHER

There can only be one individual
in each person's life
who embodies the role of nurturer to
the body, mind, and soul.

It takes a very special vessel to hold
all the responsibilities of a

"MOM" —

and that's a woman like you.

God knew all that I would need
when He gave me to you!

I appreciate you all the more now that
I'm a mom myself. I hope I can be just like
you with Johann. I miss you!
P.S. my favorite is p.22.

Love,
Bing →

39

Thank You, Lord,

for my mother. She is truly a gem of immeasurable worth.

As she has prayed for me numerous times, Lord,
I pray You will watch over her and care for her needs.
And, keep me, Dear Lord,
firm on the path she set for me so that
no matter how far I roam in life,
I'll always come back to the foundation she has laid.
Amen.